THE GRAND UNIVERSAL TAROT

Bruno de Nys

Published by REDFeather Mind, Body, Spirit
an imprint of Schiffer Publishing Ltd
4880 Lower Valley Road, Atglen, PA 19310
Phone: (610) 593-1777
Fax: (610) 593-2002

E-mail: info@redfeathermbs.com
Web: www.redfeathermbs.com/

Library of Congress Control Number: 2022932087

All rights reserved. No part of this work may be reproduced or used in any form or by any means—graphic, electronic, or mechanical, including photocopying or information storage and retrieval systems—without written permission from the publisher.

ISBN: 978-0-7643-6533-1

Printed and bound in China

© Bruno de Nys, 2003-2022 for the text of the book
© Bruno de Nys, 2005 for the Grand Universal Tarot deck
© Editions Bruno de Nys, 2022 for graphic design, illustrations, packaging (book and box), translation.

To send correspondence to the author about this deck
please contact: contact@editionsbrunodenys.com

CONTENTS

INTRODUCTION
Tarot, an intuitive and instinctive alphabet ... P.5
How to use the Grand Universal Tarot ... P.10

PART 1 – THE 22 MAJOR ARCANAS AND THEIR MAIN MEANINGS

The Magician ... P.12
The High Priestess ... P.14
The Empress ... P.16
The Emperor ... P.18
The Hierophant ... P.20
The Lovers ... P.22
The Chariot ... P.24
Justice ... P.26
The Hermit ... P.28
The Wheel of Fortune ... P.30
Strength ... P.32
The Hanged Man ... P.34
Death ... P.36
Temperance ... P.38
The Devil ... P.40
The Tower ... P.42
The Star ... P.44
The Moon ... P.46
The Sun ... P.48

CONTENTS

Judgement	P.50
The World	P.52
The Fool	P.54

PART 2 – THE MINOR ARCANAS AND THEIR GENERAL MEANINGS

Aces to the Kings	P.56

PART 3 – THE GENERIC AND THE SUBSTITUTE CARDS

Work	P.78
Finances	P.79
Emotion	P.79
Health	P.79
Making the cards speak: phrasing	P.80

PART 4 – READINGS

THE CUT READING	P.83
The simple cut	P.84
One level cut	P.85
One level cut architecture and time	P.86
Examples	P.87
THE CROSS READING	P.90
Cross draw architecture	P.91
Examples	P.92

ABOUT THE AUTHOR

	P.96

I - TAROT, AN INTUITIVE AND INSTINCTIVE ALPHABET

For many centuries, the Tarot has been at the service of humanity. Long reserved for «insiders», this tool for getting to know yourself and others is accessible to us today.

Tarot is now part of our daily landscape in most societies and cultures. However, the origin of this magnificent tool is not really known. The Tarot has undergone many changes in its history, in form, not in substance. It «mutated» in order to adapt to the various political and religious events of the times. It often came close to vanishing. It survived, however, thanks to its magnificent ability to adapt.

Intelligently designed, this alphabet easily made the transition from academic language to street talk. It has seduced and resonated with people from all classes of society, who in turn have used it openly or occultly.

Today, this resonance is confirmed: The Tarot always responds to the deepest philosophical and psychological questions that human beings ask themselves. The Tarot, like a sumptuous fresco, depicts the great energetic currents as well as the great aspirations or trials that each human being may experience during his earthly journey.

It is not divine, it is a visual, numerical and instinctive alphabet. Our ancestors passed it on with intelligence, brotherhood and acumen. It is a wonderful compilation of the feelings and stages of life that every human can or should experience throughout their existence.

Everything is there: birth, learning, parents, children, work, love, hate, manipulation, sexuality, power, psychology, brotherhood, hope, health, luck, death, revelation, the future, spirituality... nothing that is human seems to escape the Tarot...!

The Tarot is like a road map that allows us to find our path again each time we feel unsure. Its magic (in the noble sense of the term) is that it can, at any point in time, provide answers to each of our existential questions: present, future and sometimes even past. It brings people together in a common language, with a better understanding of ourselves and others. It soothes anxieties because it warns of the forces in action in all situations. It unifies. It erases social, educational, and cultural bounderies. It reminds us there is more to our humanity than skin color, race, or religion ... Tarot becomes universal ...

For Tarot lovers, all the decks created during the last few centuries—whether by insiders, fanatics or even novices —deserve respect. They contribute, sometimes modestly, to the spreading of this universal alphabet. The Tarot is a universe in perpetual movement. To try to freeze it definitively would not make sense.

The Grand Universal Tarot is the result of years of work and observation. It is an easy tool to use, pleasant to the touch and durable over time. It will suit adepts and beginners alike. It visually respects the tradition of the ancient Tarots: painted by hand and representing characters evolving in colorful scenes and symbolic landscapes.

The Grand Universal Tarot gives a new dimension to this tool: the imagination is stimulated more quickly, and the vibrant colors and scenes invite spontaneity and intuition!

Using the Tarot for clairvoyance and projection

Generations of thinkers conceived and created the Tarot through observation, intuition, much experiment and much trial and error. The Tarot is a vast compilation of ideas and human life experiences originally represented by 22 arcanas known as "Majors." Much later, it was expanded by adding "Minor Arcanas." It took centuries for the Tarot to evolve into its current size of 78 cards.

One only needs to try Tarot to see what a perfect tool it is. Useful in psychology (its primary funtion) and for understanding events, it is actually the tool most used by clairvoyants and mediums.

But any sensitive, intuitive and curious person can use the Tarot to practice clairvoyance.

You just need to know a few basic rules and never forget them:

- never use Tarot to impress the crowd.

- do not use this tool to control others.

- do not live your life based on a Tarot reading. You must remain in control of your life.

- keep your readings simple and accessible (words, attitude).

- do not assert, but suggest the messages.

2 - HOW TO USE THE GRAND UNIVERSAL TAROT

The purpose of this book is to familiarize you with the Tarot and to access the main Tarot-related mechanisms that will provide quick answers to all your questions.

The cards are only read in the upright position. Each card has a positive (+) and a negative (-) meaning.

To know whether the meaning of the card is favorable or challenging, you need to identify its position in your draw.

In the CUT draw, the card positioned on the left will take a positive meaning (+) and the card positioned on the right, a negative meaning (-).

In the CROSS draw, it is necessary to give deeper thought to your analysis, and consider the surrounding arcanas before delivering the positive or negative meaning of the Tarot message.

Finally, you should know that traditionally, the major arcanas also represent characters or specific professions.

For example: The High Priestess represents the grandmother... but this arcana can also refer to people who work in research or teaching.

A good understanding of all these elements will allow you to quickly obtain excellent results.

Remember: The Tarot is an instinctive, visual, and emotional tool. It is also logical. But the more you intellectualize it, the less acurate your results will be.
So... try and apply simplicity, curiosity, intuition and clarity in a relaxed environment.

Let's now study the major arcanas of the Grand Universal Tarot.

I - THE 22 MAJOR ARCANAS AND THEIR MAIN MEANINGS

I - THE MAGICIAN

**YOUTH. RECKLESSNESS.
ABILITY TO ADAPT.
START-UP.**

Its presence always brings freshness, optimism and contagious dynamism. However, you must always observe the cards that surround The Magician to understand its full meaning since on its own it does not give a precise message.

When in a challenging position, The Magician represents a lack of preparation and thought that can cause disagreement. Making important decisions is not recommended. It is also indicative of a lack of consistency or work required to achieve results.

Characters: Children under 10 years old. Artists, dancers, freelance workers (close to The Hierophant), smooth talkers. Magicians, start-ups, newborns (when close to The World).

Positive meaning (+): Novelty. Hope. The beginning of events. Innovation. Opportunism. The ability to seduce. Professionally, this is a good time to seek new employment opportunities and dare to take initiatives. Money is used for hobbies and fun; financial resources are limited. Your romantic life is dominated by a playful attitude, and a time of mutual self-discovery.

Negative meaning (-): Immaturity. Bad starts. Laziness. Lies (with The High Priestess). Lack of experience. Illusions. Fear of taking initiatives or making a mistake. Lack of professional experience or specialized studies (with The High Priestess). Be wary of impulsive spending, the risk of getting into debt is real. Your emotional life lacks stability, you don't know what you really want.

Astrological association: Aries

II - THE HIGH PRIESTESS

KNOWLEDGE. INITIATION. CONSCIENTIOUSNESS. SECRETS.

She brings a lot of depth, wisdom and important consideration to the draw. Her presence indicates that it is good to reflect and observe. Your experience and your achievements will work to your advantage.

In a challenging position in a draw, you will have the unpleasant feeling that you do not have complete understanding of the situation, that something is hidden and preventing you from finding the solution. It is sometimes the indication of a conspiracy, a betrayal, a disillusion or a deception.

Characters: Women over 75. Mother, grandmothers. Writers (with The Empress). Researchers. Mediums. Religious. The mistress or the lover. Midwives (when with The Hermit). School teachers. Meticulous people.

Positive meaning (+): Studies. Mind. Analysis. Calm and, discretion. Psychology. Intuition, clairvoyance. Pregnancy (with The Hermit). Good period for training courses or apprenticeships of all kinds. Efficient financial management thanks to your analytical mind. Searching for a stable and cerebral love relationship.

Negative meaning (-): Withdrawal. Heartlessness, resentment. Hypocrisy. The unspoken. Jealousy. Deceit. Adultery (with The Devil). Lack of knowledge or culture in a particular field. Loneliness (with The Hermit or The Hanged Man). Lack of self-confidence (with The Star). Depression (with The Moon or The Tower). Greed.

There is no astrological association.

III - THE EMPRESS

**INTELLIGENCE.
COMMUNICATION.
CHARM AND SEDUCTION.
FEMININE ENERGY.**

The Empress is an active card; she represents the sharpness of mind and clear ideas. In a draw, she indicates the determination to follow through with one's ambitions.

Her unfavorable aspects are stubbornness and sometimes vanity, which will stand in the way of achievement. Projects will often be delayed. Loss of self-confidence is common (especially for a woman).

Characters: The seeker. Women between 25 and 75 years old. Spouses. Female directors. Court officials. Psychologists. Writers. Engineers. Teachers. Scholars. Reporters and journalists (with The Fool).

Positive meaning (+): Written works. Letters and positive responses. Successful job searches. Elegance. Education. An above-average intelligence (with The High Priestess). Will-power. Fertility. Generosity. Optimism. The power of persuasion. Self-awareness. Your intellectual thinking is of high quality, your speech is good, go for it! Now is a good time to progress in a professional career. If you are looking for work, this is a lucky time for finding a job. Finances are smartly managed. In a relationship or single, you are able to seduce and conquer very easily. Your romantic relationships are harmonious.

Negative meaning (-): Miscommunication. Misplaced ego. Pretension or loss of self-confidence (especially for a woman). Utopias. Projects are delayed. Your work no longer stimulates you. Female rivalries are possible. Period of whims, beware of unnecessary expenses. Excess of mental thinking ends up harming the couple, pride must give way to communication. Single people prefer frivolity.

Astrological association: Virgo

IIII - THE EMPEROR

STABILITY. AUTHORITY. REALIZATION. SECURITY. MALE ENERGY.

His presence indicates great working strength, determination and discipline. A yearning for what is tangible and constructive. The Emperor clearly shows that you have the capacity and the tenacity to achieve your ambitions.

In a challenging position, he indicates (especially for a man) a lack of self-confidence. You will have a feeling of rigidity, numerous limitations or material difficulties. Much effort will have to be made to obtain a satisfactory result. Beware of a tendency to overthink or be closed minded.

Characters: Men between 25 and 75 years old and more generally, male seekers. Fathers, fathers-in-law. Decision-makers. Willing and hard-working people. Businessmen (with The Devil).

Positive meaning (+): Positive authority. The bases, the roots, the foundations. The ego. The power of work. The substance. Constructive actions. Your mind is forthright and structured. The sense of reality. Good period for asserting yourself or finding a job. In your profession, your sense of realities and responsibilities is recognized (especially for a man). Financial stability and long-term projects. Stable sentimental life. A real estate purchase project can be considered (with The Moon). Possibility of meeting a partner in the professional environment (with The Chariot).

Negative meaning (-): Stubbornness. Temporary material worries (with The Devil), bad habits. Breaking of contracts (with Justice). Dishonesty. Male chauvinism. Lack of self-confidence (especially for a man). Possible loss of employment (with Death), there is a lot of antagonism in your professional environment. Money or work problems harm the couple, beware of excessive jealousy and possessiveness.

Astrological association: Taurus

V - THE HIEROPHANT

WISDOM. BLESSING. UNIONS. CONSCIENCE. PROTECTION. SPECIALIZATION.

The Hierophant reassures and calms the reading, he allows the situation to be viewed with clarity. He symbolizes a serious and effective approach to the subject in hand. His presence provides beneficial support.

When in a challenging position in a draw, you are off to a bad start; you may not have enough assets in hand. Expect difficulties and project postponements. You will need to exercise patience, wisdom and show self-sacrifice before things work out. Beware of unproductive stubbornness because you might clash with those who have more power than you.

Characters: Men over 75 years old. Specialists of all kinds. Grandfathers. Teachers. Philosophers. Lecturers. Gifted people. Priests. Doctors (with The Hanged Man).

Farmers (with Death). All liberal professions. Certified technicians, engineers.

Positive meaning (+): Teaching. Spirituality. Religions. Good advice. Natural authority. Forgiveness. The sense of duty. Psychology. Problem solving. Contracts (with Justice). You reap the fruits of your work, stability and good financial mentality. Couple will experience a blissful period. Marriage (with Justice).

Negative meaning (-): Severity. Bigotry. Bad advice. Intolerance. Lack of specializations. Your outward appearance gives others a bad impression of you. Temporary financial limitations. A gradual tearing apart of the couple due to routine. Divorce (with Justice).

There is no astrological association.

VI - THE LOVERS

LOVE. CHOICES. DOUBTS. LIGHT-HEADEDNESS. ADOLESCENCE.

Most of the time, The Lovers' optimism describes situations that are pleasant to experience. He intervenes in events that are more or less limiting. Love or friendship often takes precedence. This arcana indicates that the seeker has a positive approach concerning the questions asked.

When challengingly positioned in a draw, The Lovers create doubt and uncertainty. The emotional side of life is often weakened or negative. There is a lack of assertiveness in your professional field, or your daily work doesn't please or no longer pleases you. Your financial management lacks discipline and spending, sometimes futile, creates problems that could have been avoided with better forethought.

Characters: Teenagers. Anyone who is in love. Seducers and seductresses. People in contact with the public. Artists. Presenters (radio or TV with Temperance).

Positive meaning (+): Sincerity, openness to others. Beauty, charm. Enthusiasm. A period of multiple choices. A pleasant professional journey where new things are learned. Bodily pleasures. It's a good time to meet people, and for easy and enjoyable seduction. If you're in a relationship, everything is going well. A positive and relaxed period.

Negative meaning (-): Worry. Excessive shyness. Uncertainty. Your love life may be difficult. Lack of love. Jealousy. A feeling of emotional abandonment. Loss of confidence in others. Laziness. Bad exam results or unsuccessful interviews (especially with Judgement). You don't know whichcareer to take up or you don't like your job anymore. Expenses are too high; you should avoid taking out a loan.

There is no astrological association.

VII- THE CHARIOT

WORK. SUCCESS. JOURNEYS. SPEED.

His presence always brings optimism, dynamism and frequently indicates success, especially in the domain of work, finance, and also seduction.

When in a challenging position, you will feel like things are not moving forward, no matter how hard you try. Difficulties or slowdowns in the workplace can cause anxiety and errors of judgement. Be wary of impatience, remain calm in order to avoid disappointment.

Characters: Salespeople. Conquerors. Automobile and mechanical professionals (with The Wheel of Fortune). Ambassadors (with The World). Altruistic and charitable people (with The Hanged Man). Racing drivers (with Strength). Very active characters. Professional trainers (with The Hierophant or Justice).

Positive meaning (+): Travel. Success. Talent. A very good indicator that you are going to find work. Rapid evolution. A good period financially, the purchase of a vehicle can be considered. Money is earned through personal merit and perseverance. Projects or ideas make progress. Luck. Love conquests become easier, you are a seductress or a seducer, perceived to be a good sentimental and sensuous match. Couples are harmonious.

Negative meaning (-): Pride and failure. Willpower alone is not strong enough. If you are looking for work, more must be done. Be careful of risky trips by car (with The Tower or Death). The recovery period for eventual financial shortfalls will be long. A lack of frankness, you should open yourself up to others more. For single people, the emotional side of a relationship is not a priority and thus relationships lack consistency. You should not focus on your professional concerns as this can prove harmful to your relationship.

Astrological association: Sagittarius

VIII- JUSTICE

BALANCE. LEGAL AREAS. ADMINISTRATION. RIGIDITY.

A symbol of discipline and fair perspective, Justice brings great stability but also a certain coldness. Its message is direct and relentless. The advice is clear and very rational, it will often tell you that you are on the right track.

In the challenging position in the draw, it indicates major oppositions that work against you or against your questions. This strictness leaves no room for doubt, and much less so for levity. In such a position, Justice often symbolizes a harsh intellectual approach or bad management of the subject matter in hand. Difficulties can be overcome as long as you question yourself.

Characters: Lawyers. Judges. Accountants. Managers. Government officials. Anyone with a fixed and well-established job. The government (with The Devil). The police (with Strength). The army (with The Devil).

Positive meaning (+): Justice as a whole. Rationale. Reasoning. Contracts of all types (especially with The Hierophant). Stability. Intellectual rigor. Discipline. A good indicator that you are ready to take civil service examinations (with The High Priestess). Finances are well managed. You are looking for a stable emotional life but it would be beneficial to allow a little more space for fun.

Negative meaning (-): Psychological rigidity or lack of discipline. Disorder. You have to learn to question yourself. Above all, you should not initiate legal proceedings. Bad contracts (especially with The Hierophant). Administrative difficulties. Finances are limited and it is not advisable to take out a loan. Emotional coldness within couples. Divorce (with The Hierophant). You don't want to embark on a new romance, you prefer loneliness to possible disappointment.

Astrological association: Libra

VIIII - THE HERMIT

TIME. SLOWNESS. OLD AGE. CONCEPTION OR THE END OF THINGS. PERSEVERANCE. SERIOUSNESS.

Often disliked, The Hermit, nonetheless offers a very beautiful psychological and philosophical outlook on life. Things move slowly but surely. Projects are built on healthy and solid foundations. This is a guarantee of success for the future. You are on the right track; persistence will eventually yield great results.

When in a challenging position in a draw, this card causes a feeling of isolation and highlights difficulties in communicating your feelings or emotions. You may be very shy or have the impression that your past is holding you back. Ultimately, this position evokes great slowness, which is often difficult to live with ...

Characters: Monks. Wise people. Researchers. The elderly, people over 90 years old. All professions that require attention to detail, calm and long-term evolution. People who work closely with the elderly or death (associated with Death). Midwives (associated with The Hierophant).

Positive meaning (+): Time does its work. Courage. Concentration. Soul. Voluntary solitude. Periods of structuring. Long-term goals. Your professional experience is a great asset. A sense of economy and financial stability, however, large investments should be avoided. Conscientiousness. Friendly and sentimental loyalty. Pregnancy (with The High Priestess).

Negative meaning (-): Greed. Stubbornness. Excessive shyness. Reluctant acceptance of loneliness. Withdrawal from others. You should confront the world more. An outward appearance that is sometimes unflattering or not understood by others. Lack of sexual drive (with The Devil). Mistrust of youth and new things. Over conservative attitudes. Long periods of emotional drought. Major delays.

Astrological association: Capricorn

X - THE WHEEL OF FORTUNE

FORTHCOMING EVENTS. SEASONS. CYCLES. DESTINY. LUCK.

The Wheel of Fortune brings a notion of movement and sometimes speed to a draw. However, this card is something of a chameleon because its meaning changes form when in contact with other cards. Therefore, the surrounding environment will always be the key to fully understanding its true meaning. The Wheel of Fortune is optimistic and tells you that your plans or your expectations are going to work. You approach situations with great intellectual flexibility and heightened ability to adapt to them.

When in a challenging position, you get the unpleasant feeling that events are beyond your control, and that you are unable to take full action. Delays and setbacks are frequent. It also often represents a reluctance to act and be bold.

Characters: Inventors. Adventurers. Travelers. Astrologers (with The Star). Mechanics (with The Chariot). Stock exchange traders (with The Devil).

Positive meaning (+): Life cycles. The future. Rapid changes. A good time for risk-taking. The unexpected. Inventiveness. A good time to boost your professional career. Finances fluctuate temporarily but without worrying you. A rich period for many romantic encounters and if you are in a relationship, everything is progressing as it should.

Negative meaning (-): Roadblocks that you can't explain. A lack of enthusiasm to drive your own abilities. Stagnation. Sloppiness. Negligence. Adversity. Bohemian tendencies. Projects are poorly structured and fall behind schedule. External events have too much influence on you. A risk of accidents at work (with The Chariot or The Tower). Financial instability and recklessness. Romantic encounters at risk to lose interest.

There is no astrological association.

XI - STRENGTH

CONTROL OF SITUATIONS. COURAGE. SELF-CONFIDENCE.

Strength indicates that you have all the potential necessary to succeed. It symbolizes a period of physical and intellectual dynamism. Its presence in a draw leans toward success thanks to the appropriateness of your actions.

In a challenging position, you risk failing to master situations. Be careful not to waste too much energy unnecessarily, you expose yourself to great physical and psychological fatigue. Power balance relationships may exist with your close or distant acquaintances. Be careful not to lack diplomacy and be wary of impatience colored with aggression.

Characters: All people who carry out a dangerous profession. Organizers. Removal men (with The Tower). Animal trainers. Firefighters (with The Tower).

Healers (with Temperance). All people who succeed thanks to their art. Sports people.

Positive meaning (+): The power of fulfilment. Self-made success. A good time to start your own business (with The Hierophant). Productivity. Wise judgements. Self-control. An ideal time to take risks in all areas. Financial management and generosity. A well-balanced sexuality (with The Devil), harmonious couples; if you are single, a major encounter may cross your path.

Negative meaning (-): Impatience. Anger. Violence. Jealousy, tyranny. No command over external factors: you feel overwhelmed. You should not rush things. Risks of bankruptcy (with Justice). Power struggles in relationships with your colleagues or your superiors. Be careful not to overspend. Concerns about sexuality (with The Devil), a battle of nerves within couples.

Astrological association: Leo

XII - THE HANGED MAN

HEALTH. SPIRITUALITY. BENEFICIAL WAITING PERIODS. ACCEPTANCE.

The Hanged Man shows stability and favours the continuity of what you are experiencing. Bad surprises are rare and most of the time they are well managed, thanks to your patience and your flexible mind.

When this card is in a challenging position, you will have a very unpleasant feeling of blockage. This can come from external events but most often you are responsible for what happens. Your lack of action, a temporary physical and psychological fatigue as well as a momentary inaction, can explain the current situation. You refuse to accept realities and to face the facts. With The Hanged Man in this challenging position, it is very rare that you see things as they truly are.

Characters: Priests. The enlightened. Slaves. Patriots. Devoted friends. The spiritual brother. Weak spirited. The unemployed. Herbalists. Mediums. Alcoholics. Tramps. Humanitarian associations. All people who give their energy to serve others. Health workers.

Positive meaning (+): It is the card symbolizing health. Temporary setbacks. Letting go. Humanism. Professional or emotional ties. Dedication. Initiation. Self-sacrifice. Fraternity. Financial limitations are temporary and accepted. Friendships are important to you. Your couple is stable, loyal and respectful. Even if your professionnal life seems in a rut, it is not a good time to take risks. It is preferable to choose stability and continuity.

Negative meaning (-): Little or no taste for action. Real blockages. Depression (with The Moon or The Fool). Mysticism. Resignation. Momentarily frail health. Unhealthy lifestyle. The need for psychological help (with The Moon or The Fool).

Astrological association: Pisces

XIII-DEATH (CARD WITHOUT A NAME)

RADICAL AND UNAVOIDABLE TRANSFORMATION. HONOR. HONESTY. RENEWAL.

Often not liked because of its unattractive image, this card is systematically involved in the unblocking of situations and the progress of projects. With Death everything becomes fluid, clear and precise. This card represents anyone who gives themselves the means to achieve their goals; it's the hard work that pays off.

In a challenging position, this card indicates that you are undergoing an event or a situation against your will. To avoid difficulties, you will need a lot of fortitude and work, otherwise you risk the destruction of your material or emotional stability. Contrary to popular beliefs and its iconography, this card alone does not indicate death.

Characters: Ancestors. Widows and widowers. Farmers (with The Hierophant), biomass. Bailiffs (with Justice). Chemists. Psychics who commune with spirits. Psychoanalysts (with The High Priestess). Surgeons (with The Hierophant). Trades connected to death (with The Hermit). People who work in criminology. Forensic specialists. Radiologists. IT (information technology).

Positive meaning (+): Great changes. Integrity. Rebirth. Fidelity. Hard work. Good period to change jobs (particularly close to The Chariot). The sense of effort, saving money and responsibilities. Perfectionism. The end of loneliness thanks to a sudden encounter (with The Lovers); the couple acts to break the patterns of routine.

Negative meaning (-): Failure. Pessimism. Aridity, an emotional dry period. Changes are badly experienced or unwanted. A bad time to make decisions. Low spirit (with The Moon or The Fool). Greed (with The Hermit). Possible depression due to financial worries. Difficulties to seduce and to enhance one's image. The end of a love (with The Lovers). Likened to having a heart of stone.

There is no astrological association.

XIIII-TEMPERANCE

COMMUNICATION. REST. HOLIDAYS. FRATERNITY. NEGOTIATION.

This card symbolizes the restarting of a situation or the reunion or comeback of a person. Temperance is the first Angel of the Tarot. It offers a path of wisdom, respect, spirituality and gentleness. It encourages reflection and calm. Its presence delivers a message of hope and confidence. It is useless to force the situations, the expected events will eventually happen.

In a challenging position, you have to accept a slow pace and cultivate prudence. You don't communicate enough. Indecision slows down projects or encounters. Influences from the past can upset you and create doubt and inaction.

Characters: Publicists. Film directors. Men of broadcasting (with Judgement). Natural therapies (close to The

Hanged Man or The Star). Travel agents (when with The World). Electricians. Plumbers. Musicians (with Judgement). Healers (with The Devil). All professions related to gentleness and communication. Internet and social networks.

Positive meaning (+): Leisure. Openness to others. Respect for your body and its energies. Trust. Value of negotiation. The quiet strength. Very good communication, diplomacy (especially with The Star). Good professional period, favorable to contact or help professions. The money can be used for leisure or travel (with The World or The Fool), even with moderate finances. Possible romantic adventures or the return of a story from the past (with The Lovers). Couples are calm and harmonious. Tenderness.

Negative meaning (-): Fatigue. Nervous tensions (with The Devil). Bad influences, manipulation. Too much hesitation leads to inertia. Lack of drive at work. Temporary laziness. Too much spending, despite low finances. Emotional inconsistency causing dependence and passivity toward people or situations. Too much submission to the partner. Useless withdrawal.

Astrological association: Aquarius.

XV-THE DEVIL

MONEY. POWER. CUNNING. SEXUALITY. SEDUCTION.

The desire to act in a clear and definitive way in all areas. The devouring will. The ability to convince.
Your physical and intellectual magnetism will operate favorably. You have a sense of power and self-assurance that nothing and no one can stand in your way. You feel invested with an energy of success and conquest and you will inevitably find an audience to follow you. You will not hesitate to use all your charms to achieve your goals.

When The Devil is in a challenging position, you will have the impression that your problems are growing, without being able to find a coherent solution at the moment. It is a phase of various tensions, of aggressiveness. Emotionally, you can experience disagreeable situations, encounter problems as a couple. The lack of desire explains a badly managed or badly experienced sexuality.

Financial difficulties are temporarily aggravated, it is important not to take risks. You may experience anxiety and uncertainty.

Characters: Bankers (with The Hierophant), businessmen and women (with The Chariot). Athletes (with Strength). Thieves. Politicians (with Justice). Hypnosis (with The High Priestess). Healers (with Temperance). Wizards (with Death). Actors (with The Star), Idols (with The World). Secret organizations, sects (with The High Priestess).

Positive meaning (+): Good financial times through intense activity and hard work. Salary increases. Passion. Multiple encounters. The couple needs adrenaline to function well. Instinct, physical vitality. Ability to persuade. The strategies, the will to dominate. Impatience. Strong magnetism.

Negative meaning (-): Brutality (of words or deeds), material problems, anger. Selfishness. Destructive sentimental passions. Mental manipulations, abuse of power. Stress at work. Bad dating. Drugs, alcohol (especially with The Moon or The Fool). Thefts, trafficking, lies, corruption, adultery (with The High Priestess).

Astrological association: Scorpio

XVI-THE TOWER

AWARENESS. VOLUNTARY DEMOLITIONS. CHALLENGES. SALUTARY CRISES.

This card encourages boldness. Its message: dare to shake things up. It's the Champagne bottle of the Tarot! If you do not like inertia and slowness, The Tower will serve you well! Its presence evokes dynamic energy, renewal, favorable risk-taking. It indicates that it is good to demolish, on the condition of rebuilding on new foundations.

If in a challenging position in the draw, it indicates ambitions that may collapse, overestimation of a situation or insufficient ability to manage an event. Setbacks (financial, emotional or professional) are frequent and it is good for you to question yourself. Depression and discouragement are possible (with The Moon or The High Priestess).

Characters: Builders. Architects. Psychiatrists (with The Fool). Physically handicapped (with The Chariot). Astronauts (with The Star). Terrorists. Firefighters. People taking calculated risks. Bee keepers. Electricians (with The Chariot or The Hierophant).

Positive meaning (+): A conscious determination, a good time to try in all areas. Finances are on the rise again, investments in real estate are wise. Structural changes. Brilliant innovations (with The Fool). Temporary work (with Temperance). Moving (with The Moon), construction and evolution. Love at first sight (with The Sun). Sudden and favorable meeting (with The Lovers). The couple builds on solid foundations.

Negative meaning (-): Delusions of grandeur. Downfall of strategies and projects. Possibility of layoff or bankruptcy (with Justice), be careful. Dark thoughts. Pride. Bad time to take financial risks, reversals of fortune can occur. Risk of fires or domestic accidents (with The Moon). Break ups (with Death). The partners no longer understand each other.

There is no astrological association.

XVII-THE STAR

LUCK. PEACE. HOPE. THE BODY. GENEROSITY. THE FUTURE.

The Star indicates that you will soon be rewarded: luck is on your side! Any conflicts subside because your natural optimism allows you to approach the future positively.

In a challenging position, it means you will have to wait before getting what you want, but this will not bother you since you know how to wait calmly, you intuitively feel that everything will eventually happen. The Star can sometimes indicate a lack of self-confidence at the bodily level. These doubts are unjustified and they will not last over time. There is every reason to hope for a future improvement.

Characters: Artists. Poets. Musicians (with Judgement). The principle of feminine and masculine beauty. Landscape artists. Ecology. Biological farmers (with Death).

People in a harmonious relationship with nature. Renewable energies, alternative medicine (with The Hierophant). Psychics.

Positive meaning (+): The arts (with The Sun), your creative spirit. Purity. Friendship. The natural. Simplicity. Beauty. Acceptance of and respect for your body. Good time to start a diet. Humanism. Humility. Patience. Good atmosphere at work, thanks to your kindness. Despite financial limitations, you prefer giving and helping, rather than receiving. Love and trust in the couple. If you are alone, many people like you, look around you a little more...!

Negative meaning (-): The Star does not indicate failure but delays, often out of a sense of nonchalance in the face of events. Professional projects are postponed. If you are looking for work, act because you rely too much on "your lucky star." In the same way, money doesn't fall from the sky... If the couple is going through a difficult period, the situation will soon get better. Singles are waiting for love but for the moment they prefer friendship.

There is no astrological association.

XVIII-THE MOON

FAMILY. THE HOUSING. THE UNCONSCIOUS. DREAMS. THE EMOTIONS. CHILDHOOD. THE PAST.

This card sometimes complicates the interpretation because it is rich in concrete but also subtle meanings, often strong emotionally. The Moon symbolizes sensitivity, emotionality, psychology and altruism. Great acts or beautiful ideas can arise from this phase of positive creativity and curiosity. Family and friends mean a lot, they are an emotional landmark.

In a challenging position, The Moon expresses a strong uncertainty, a difficulty in dissociating fantasy from reality. Anxieties. It can also warn of psychological concerns or depression. The positive part of the spread must be strong to compensate.

Other main general meanings: Imagination. Home. Public places. Crowds. Winter. Night. The north. The ocean.

House moving (with The Tower). Hospitals (with The Hanged Man). The family business.

Characters: Navigators (with The Chariot). Fishermen (with Death). Barmen. Night jobs. Creative people. Historians. Estate agents and builders (with The Hierophant). DJs (with Judgement). Hoteliers (with The World). Prison staff (with The Tower) and hospital staff (with The Hanged Man).

Positive meaning (+): The opportunities at work are numerous and your originality seduces. An ideal time to invest in real estate. Financial assistance from the family is possible. Couples look to upgrade their home. Singles can meet many people during outings, especially in the evenings with friends.

Negative meaning (−): Fears. Drugs or alcohol (with The Devil or The Fool). Flight from reality. Family worries. Nervous breakdown. Bad sleep. Deceptions (with The High Priestess). Distrust. Emotional blackmail. The fear of suffering hinders encounters. Escape from professional responsibilities, you no longer like your job but you do not give yourself the means to change. Finances are unreliable, watch out for unpleasant surprises.

Astrological association: Cancer.

XVIIII - THE SUN

PERSONAL RADIATION. THE EGO. CHILDREN. THE COUPLE. THE PRESENT.

Its presence is stimulating and will give you the feeling that thanks to your energy, everything will succeed for you. Your positive energy is communicative and your optimism is foolproof ! Thanks to the joy it brings, The Sun allows a beautiful lucidity with all the present situations.

Challengingly positioned, The Sun will cause delays and force you to be more down to earth. It can hurt your ego and heighten your touchiness. However, it is wiser to agree to postpone your many and sometimes too ambitious projects.

Other main general meanings: Love of children, physical beauty, summer, the day, the south.

Characters: Children. Cardiologists (with The Hierophant). Solar energy specialists (with The Hierophant).

Fashion designers (with The World or The Fool). Close-knit couples. Everyone who knows how to convince with their eloquent speech (with Judgement) or by their physical assets (with The Star). Beauty and luxury trades (with The Star). Teachers (with The High Priestess or The Hierophant).

Positive meaning (+): Good vitality, self-awareness. The present. The chance to seize. Optimism. Your artistic gifts can be recognized (with The Star). Good period to find work or to obtain responsibilities (with The Chariot or The Devil). Finances are up, attraction to beautiful things. A harmonious and faithful couple, children bring many joys. If you are single, your radiance attracts attention, meetings are facilitated. Love at first sight is possible (with The Tower).

Negative meaning (-): Susceptibility, vanity, pride plays tricks, tendency to believe that everything is due to you. Lack of dynamic energy, fatigue. If you are working or looking for a job, it is good to be less proud and more modest. Watch out for overspending (especially with The Devil), finances are down. The couple lacks energy, you have to react. Singles should be more humble and approachable.

Astrological association: Gemini

XX - JUDGEMENT

LISTENING. COMMUNICATION. THE OBLIGATIONS. THE SOUND. INSPIRATION.

Judgement is a serious card. It is preferable to analyze its message carefully, or be subject to serious disappointment. It shows only one way forward, with no other options. It speeds up events and promotes communication. This presence always indicates dynamism, ease of speech and an expansion phase.

In a challenging position in the draw, it will frequently mean a failure in the area studied or very great efforts to be made to obtain satisfaction. It is often an indicator of a lack of communication and open-mindedness. It's a difficult period; external events can play against you.

Other main general meanings: The public. Modernity. Music. Social relations. Signs of fate.

Characters: Professions related to the public. Marketing. Candidates for an election (with The Devil or Temperance).

Sound engineers (with The Hierophant). Singers. Musicians. Inventors (with The Fool). Journalists. Speech therapists (with The Hierophant). Wind power specialists (with The Hierophant). Judges (with Justice). Aircraft pilots (with The Chariot).

Positive meaning (+): Sudden and well-thought-out actions. The difficulties do not last. Spirituality. The obligation to do something specific. Legal successes. Boldness at work, energetic period. Seriousness and financial stability. Friendship is very important to you, quick encounters if you favor social life. Couples have a good intellectual and emotional exchange. Singles have many opportunities. Attraction to people of foreign origin (with The Fool). Couples are having a great time.

Negative meaning (-): Dashed hopes. Poor judgement. Bad news. Bad Company. We don't listen to anyone. Failing professional interviews or exams (with The Chariot or The Lovers). Concentration difficulties. Feeling of suffocation and isolation at work. If you are unemployed, you find it difficult to value your skills, assert yourself. Financial limitations are accepted. Multiple meetings but without much interest. The couple lacks intimacy because friends take up too much space.

There is no astrological association.

XXI - THE WORLD

THE SUCCESS. THE RESULT OF PROJECTS. FREEDOM. TRAVELS.

The World indicates a period of freedom of spirit as well as a beautiful self-awareness, allowing many successes. Your capacity for success is great and you achieve, without forcing, most all of your goals. The support of your friends, family or professional circle can be decisive for your success.

When challengingly positioned, The World causes a feeling of isolation and the feeling of being rejected by others. This can come from too high self-esteem, misplaced pride or difficulty in accepting one's differences. You have to make yourself accessible, don't forget it takes effort to obtain results.

Characters: All people with very easy and reassuring contact. Travel agents, tourism (with The Hierophant). Celebrities and movies (with The Sun). The media (with Judgement). Diplomats (with The Star). Astronauts (with The Wheel of Fortune or The Star). Foreigners (with The Fool).

Positive meaning (+): Total success. A period of luck. Help from influential people. Receptivity to the outside world. Trips on the continent or abroad (with The Fool). Many opportunities present themselves. Feminine and masculine energy. Business trips (with The Chariot), recognition of your talent. No problem finding work, just show up. Possible expenses for a trip (with Temperance or The Fool). Good financial period. Singles have numerous opportunities. Attraction to foreigners (with The Fool). Couples living a good life.

Negative meaning (-): Pretentiousness. Social isolation. Egocentrism. Useless worldliness (with The Sun). Thoughtlessness. A general feeling of inertia. Your social environment is not always positive. Boredom and temporary difficulties in your professional activity. Financially, it's a bad time to make big investments. Emotionally, beware of false pretenses and miscommunication as a couple.

There is no astrological association.

XXII - THE FOOL

UNEXPECTED. PRESENT TIME. GENIUS OR MADNESS. MOVEMENT.

Optimism and originality are the key words of this card. It is good to dare to take risks while assuming your differences because what may seem marginal for some could become a reference for others. The Fool is impulsive, surprising, creative, joyful. Follow your instincts, while having fun.

In a challenging position, beware of utopias and its often contradictory influence with the other arcana cards. The Fool sows doubts! It is frequently associated with the arcanas of depression (The Moon, The Devil, The Tower) or with representations of the past (The Hermit, The High Priestess, The Moon, The Hanged Man), which announces psychological draws and complicated situations.

Characters: The Fool represents humanity as a whole. The creatives. The originals. The provocateurs. Psychiatrists (with The Hierophant), the mentally ill (with

(The Hanged Man). The tramps. The travellers. Trendsetters, fashion icons (with The World or Judgement). The Inventors (with The Wheel of Fortune). The acrobats (with The Magician).

Positive meaning (+): Travel abroad. Sudden impulses. Processes that cannot be stopped. The unknown, the irrational. The sudden understanding of a situation ("Eureka!"). Favorable risk-taking (if the rest of the draw confirms it). Good period in work, follow your instinct. If you are unemployed, diversify your searches and dare everything, guaranteed results! Financial life is limited, it is wise to keep your feet on the ground. In the case of a single person, only furtive and unimportant encounters cross your path. Couples lack attention for each other, you have to react.

Negative meaning (-): The blunders. The trials. The illusions. The foolishness. Temporary depressive tendency. The risk of accident (with The Chariot or The Tower). Period of questioning in the work, bankruptcy (with Justice), delays. Lack of financial lucidity, it is necessary to react quickly. Emotional fragility, the past can slow down sentimental evolution. The partners live in different worlds of misunderstanding.

There is no astrological association.

2 - THE MINOR ARCANAS AND THEIR GENERAL MEANINGS

The Tarot is divided into two distinct universes.
First of all there are the 22 major arcanas which, as we have just seen, evoke with precision all the subjects and human concerns as well as the different characters.

Then we find the 56 lesser cards named minor arcanas which provide less important information or only small details which enrich the initial message of the major cards. This hierarchy (major/minor) is not recent, most of the old Tarot already complied with this convention.

For my part, I recommend using only the major arcanas, because they are the true «soul» of the Tarot.

If you also want to use the «minors», make sure you first understand and master the «majors», otherwise you may find it difficult to understand.

I advise you to separate the major and minor Tarot cards into two piles. At first, make your draw with the major Tarot cards. Then spread out the second pile of minor cards in front of you, draw minor cards and cover the majors ones.

By proceeding in this way the message will be clear and precise.

Whatever your choice, it is useless to fall into the sterile controversy which sometimes opposes the supporters of the major arcanas practitioners against the defenders of the major and minor arcanas.
It is by practicing that you will find your truth.

Traditionally, the minor arcanas are associated with the suits in a deck of playing cards (32 or 56 cards).

Wands are related to **clubs,** they are associated with fire and the masculine.

Cups are related to **hearts,** they are associated with water and the feminine.

Pentacles are associated with **diamonds**, they represent the earth and the feminine.

Swords refer to **spades**, they are associated with air and the masculine.

The numbered cards (from ace to 10): are concepts which, combined with major cards, can give some additional information.

The figures (Kings, Queens, Knights and Jacks) often represent characters who may possibly intervene in the draw.

ACES
The beginning. The search for realization.

of Cups	of Pentacles	of Swords	of Wands

 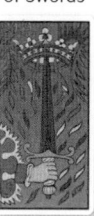 

ACE OF CUPS
<u>Positive</u>: It is the beginning of happiness. Harmony at home. Sincerity. Love.
<u>Negative</u>: A great selfishness. Hesitation in love. Emotional disillusionment.

ACE OF PENTACLES
<u>Positive</u>: Material success. Good financial life. The start of a favored business. Prosperity.
<u>Negative</u>: Greed. A lack of joy. Money and matter that do not enrich spiritually.

ACE OF SWORDS

<u>Positive</u>: Honesty. Conquest. Great strength. Very strong will. The might.
<u>Negative</u>: Lack of willpower. Pointless aggressiveness. Laziness.

ACE OF WANDS

<u>Positive</u>: Success through effort. Authority. Openness. Energy.
<u>Negative</u>: Aggression. Fatigue. Excessive agitation. Needless loss of energy.

THE TWOS

Hesitations. Dualities. Complementary or opposition.

of Cups	of Pentacles	of Swords	of Wands
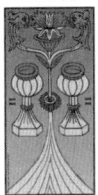		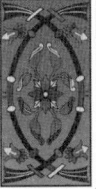	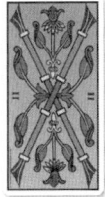

TWO OF CUPS

<u>Positive</u>: A good surprise. The end of a rivalry. Complicity. Dialogue. Dynamic couple.
<u>Negative</u>: Misunderstanding. Emotional rivalries. Separations.

TWO OF PENTACLES

<u>Positive</u>: A trip. A change of residence. The necessity to think before acting. Partnership.

<u>Negative</u>: Financial loss. Emotional instability. Delay of a project.

TWO OF SWORDS

<u>Positive</u>: A difficult choice. Uncertainty, it is necessary to assert oneself.

<u>Negative</u>: The many rivalries. Strong opposition. A bad choice. Blocked feelings.

TWO OF WANDS

<u>Positive</u>: Inevitable clashes are coming, struggles, rivalries, courage.

<u>Negative</u>: Violence, stubbornness, lack of open-mindedness.

THE THREES

The news. The mind. The inspiration. The dynamism. Short trips.

of Cups   of Pentacles   of Swords   of Wands

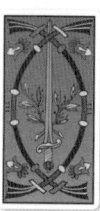

THREE OF CUPS
<u>Positive</u>: Team spirit. Favorable news arrives. A very good period of luck. Victory.
<u>Negative</u>: Poor lifestyle. Beware of abuse. Infidelity. A backward attitude. Fickleness and waste. Your friends are more important than your family and home....

THREE OF PENTACLES
<u>Positive</u>: Talent. Rising finances. Professional recognition. Bargains. Favorable associations. Promotions.
<u>Negative</u>: Pay attention to those around you, not always reliable. Indecision. Influenced.

THREE OF SWORDS
<u>Positive</u>: It is good to demolish in order to rebuild on new foundations, but you have to think before acting. Very active mind.
<u>Negative</u>: Sorrow. Wounds (especially of the soul). Jealousy. Instability. The feeling of abandonment.

THREE OF WANDS
<u>Positive</u>: Originality and talent. Vocation. Creation. Projects come to realization. Success. Recognition. Intuition.
<u>Negative</u>: Instability. Difficulties of adaptation. Lack of method.

THE FOURS

The concrete. The work. The efforts. The perseverance.
The stability or the instability.

of Cups   of Pentacles   of Swords   of Wands

FOUR OF CUPS

<u>Positive</u>: Professional and emotional stability. Consolidation of the couple.

<u>Negative</u>: Dissatisfaction with what we are currently experiencing. Doubts. Hesitations. Sentimental failure. Fear of novelty. Possessiveness. Lack of initiative. Egocentrism.

FOUR OF PENTACLES

<u>Positive</u>: Good financial management. The desire to possess materially. Sustainable investments. The desire to control everything.

<u>Negative</u>: Money can be used to manipulate others. Cupidity. Selfishness. Sizable financial worries. Real emotional conflicts due to the desire to dominate others.

FOUR OF SWORDS

<u>Positive</u>: An ordeal will end soon. A period of relaxation, fidelity.

<u>Negative</u>: Fears. Mental rigidity. Pessimism. Lack of diplomacy.

FOUR OF WANDS

<u>Positive</u>: Stability. Spontaneity. Harmony. Harvesting the fruits of one's labor. A good vitality, a good time to create something new.

<u>Negative</u>: The delay of projects. The weight of the past slows down the future. Watch out for overspending.

THE FIVES

Changes. Births. Evolution. Hindrances. Fights.

of Cups	of Pentacles	of Swords	of Wands
		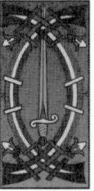	

FIVE OF CUPS

<u>Positive</u>: The end of one pattern and the beginning of another. Birth of a love story. Desire to overcome the past.

<u>Negative</u>: Emotional disappointment. Emotional breakdown. Lies. You have to agree to «lose» if you want to renew yourself.

FIVE OF PENTACLES

<u>Positive</u>: Financial stability. Business expansion. Self-confidence.
<u>Negative</u>: Job loss. Poor financial management. Feeling of exclusion. Fear of being rejected (in all areas).

FIVE OF SWORDS

<u>Positive</u>: The desire for justice. The acceptance of own limitations. Many battles have to be fought. The resumption of studies.
<u>Negative</u>: Failure and ruin. Legal problems. Bad behavior. Bad company. An unexpected friendly break-up.

FIVE OF WANDS

<u>Positive</u>: Competition. Rising to a challenge. Professional expansion. You overcome big obstacles thanks to a fighting spirit.
<u>Negative</u>: Beware of dubious contracts. Rivalries (especially professional). Multiple setbacks. Your desire to win at all costs attracts many enemies.

THE SIXES
Hesitations. Doubts. Choices. Love.
The public. Generosity.

of Cups   of Pentacles   of Swords   of Wands

SIX OF CUPS
<u>Positive</u>: Naivety and innocence. Personal fulfillment. A sentimental return from the past is possible. You recover the fruits of your efforts. The affective exchanges.
<u>Negative</u>: Disappointment. Bad emotional choices. A nostalgia that prevents you from moving forward.

SIX OF PENTACLES
<u>Positive</u>: The public. Communication. Generosity. Collaborations are favored. Financial gains.
<u>Negative</u>: Money worries. Excessive emotional submission. Debts. Bad influences.

SIX OF SWORDS

<u>Positive</u>: The end of a bad period thanks to your efforts. Health improvement. A more positive approach of life.
<u>Negative</u>: Obligatory patience. Fragile health. Frustrations.

SIX OF WANDS

<u>Positive:</u> Deserved rewards. Victory. Promotions. Good news. A search for general balance.
<u>Negative</u>: Many hesitations. Pessimism. Too much pride that isolates.

THE SEVENS
Travel. Contracts. Relationships. Goals. Victories.

of Cups	of Pentacles	of Swords	of Wands

SEVEN OF CUPS
<u>Positive</u>: Period of choice and sometimes luck. Passion. Romantic relationships or emotional encounters. Possible return of an old love.
<u>Negative</u>: Lack of self-confidence. Betrayal. Bad choices. Illusions. Laziness.

SEVEN OF PENTACLES
<u>Positive</u>: Contracts. Reaping the fruits of labor. Hard work. Financial evolution (or the resolution of financial problems). Travel.
<u>Negative</u>: Big obstacles, do not give up and be brave. Real financial worries.

SEVEN OF SWORDS
<u>Positive</u>: You can only rely on yourself. Independence. A free-thinking attitude.
<u>Negative</u>: Dishonesty. Lying and cheating. Strong opposition. Multiple blockages.

SEVEN OF WANDS
<u>Positive</u>: Courage. Achieved objectives. Professional success. Good physical and mental energy. Success.
<u>Negative</u>: Stubbornness. Aggressiveness. Unjustified anxiety. Risk of accident.

THE EIGHTS
Conflicts. Justice. Changes. Uncertainties.

| of Cups | of Pentacles | of Swords | of Wands |

EIGHT OF CUPS
<u>Positive</u>: The need for novelty. Transformation and questioning of the love life, you must accept to turn the page.
<u>Negative</u>: Emotional disillusionment. Emotional breakdown. Weakened health. Hardships.

EIGHT OF PENTACLES
<u>Positive</u>: Talent. Skill. Discipline. Patience.
<u>Negative</u>: Lack of ambition and perseverance. Debts and financial difficulties. Legal worries.

EIGHT OF SWORDS
<u>Positive</u>: Feelings are sometimes confused, beware of indecision. It is important to have confidence in yourself.

<u>Negative</u>: Isolation. Depression. Victim attitude. Fears and anxieties. The risks of illness. Physical weakness. Betrayal.

EIGHT OF WANDS

<u>Positive</u>: Travel abroad. Action. A good time to take stock of the situation. The decision to stop an activity.
<u>Negative</u>: Jealousy. Thoughtless and scattered actions. An emotional dispute. Anxieties. Susceptibility.

THE NINES

Initiation. Awareness. Concerns. Lucidity. Knowledge.

of Cups   of Pentacles   of Swords   of Wands

NINE OF CUPS

<u>Positive</u>: Period of satisfaction. The legalization of a union. The culmination of a project. Sensuality. Pleasure.
<u>Negative</u>: Betrayals. An overly epicurean approach to life. A dissolute lifestyle.

NINE OF PENTACLES
<u>Positive</u>: Success and material security. Financial investments. Signatures of contracts or notarized documents. Personal satisfaction. Independence.
<u>Negative</u>: Financial and emotional limitations. Loneliness. Postponement of projects.

NINE OF SWORDS
<u>Positive</u>: Acceptance. Fraternity. Devotion. A desirable period of slowing down, isolation and introspection: use time as an ally.
<u>Negative</u>: Worry. Aggressiveness. You can be violent or suffering yourself from violence. Pessimism. Eternal regrets. Failed acts. Blockages.

NINE OF WANDS
<u>Positive</u>: Perseverance in face of hardship. Integrity. Clear ideas. Travel. Foreign countries.
<u>Negative</u>: Lack of initiative. Naivety or on the contrary an overly defensive attitude. The fear of tomorrow.

THE TENS
The end and the beginning of a cycle. The evolution.
Challenges. Struggles. Ideals.
The quest for harmony.

of Cups   of Pentacles   of Swords   of Wands

TEN OF CUPS

<u>Positive</u>: Happiness and success. Love. Pleasures. Generosity. Harmonious health. Spirituality.

<u>Negative</u>: The emotional past blocks evolution. The end of an emotional story. The betrayal of a loved one.

TEN OF PENTACLES

<u>Positive</u>: Wealth and material evolution (especially financial). Professional promotion. A salary increase. Long-term financial investments (housing, for example). A harmonious family life.

<u>Negative</u>: Financial problems. Family worries. Excessive spending.

TEN OF SWORDS

<u>Positive</u>: Favorable legal results. Lucidity. Acceptance of difficulties. Secret preparation for a new stage.

<u>Negative</u>: Lack of action. Lack of brotherhood. Wrong choices. Negative legal outcomes.

TEN OF WANDS

<u>Positive</u>: Unplanned trips. Struggles to succeed. Physical vitality. Achievements through hard work.
<u>Negative:</u> Lack of leisure and rest. Overwork. Power struggles in relationships with your superiors at work. The burden of education.

THE PAGES

Changes. Action. Logic. Work.
Stability or instability. The young people.

of Cups	of Pentacles	of Swords	of Wands

PAGE OF CUPS

<u>Positive</u>: Sensitivity. Melancholy. The beginning of a romantic relationship. Friends. Imagination and creativity.
<u>Negative</u>: Useless daydreams. Love rivalry. Flirtations without a future. Lack of self-confidence and lack of action.

PAGE OF PENTACLES

<u>Positive</u>: New projects. The will to succeed, you give yourself the means to succeed. The good news. The help of others.
<u>Negative</u>: Sensitivity. Withdrawal. Vanity. Expenses that endanger financial stability.

PAGE OF SWORDS

<u>Positive</u>: Diplomacy. Dexterity and mental alertness. Experience.
<u>Negative</u>: Manipulation. Opposition. Financial worries with government services (tax for example). Deception.

PAGE OF WANDS

<u>Positive</u>: Courage. Loyalty. Confidence. Inspiration. New directions. Favorable risk-taking. Writings.
<u>Negative</u>: Naivety. The lack of knowledge causes errors in judgement.

THE KNIGHTS

Dynamism. Impatience. Novelty. Frankness. Determination. The quickness of events.

of Cups	of Pentacles	of Swords	of Wands

KNIGHT OF CUPS

<u>Positive:</u> Intellectual refinement. A new emotional encounter. Romanticism. A good lover or a sensual mistress.
<u>Negative</u>: Unfriendliness. Deception. Susceptibility. Idealism.

KNIGHT OF PENTACLES

<u>Positive</u>: Perseverance. Prudence and wisdom. Sense of responsibility. Loyalty.
<u>Negative:</u> Fear of taking risks. Difficulties in making sentimental choices. Pessimism. Idleness.

KNIGHT OF SWORDS

<u>Positive</u>: The increased pace of life. Courage. The ability to quickly solve a problem. The aptitude to persuade.
<u>Negative</u>: Health concerns. Sentimental coldness. Brutality. Anger.

KNIGHT OF WANDS

<u>Positive</u>: Moving. Traveling abroad. Impatience. The unexpected. The taste for adventure
<u>Negative:</u> Professional conflicts. Legal difficulties. Insensitivity to emotions. Bragging.

THE QUEENS

Communication. Advice. Devotion. Loyalty. Intelligence.
The querent, the wife or the concubine.

of Cups  of Pentacles  of Swords  of Wands

QUEEN OF CUPS

<u>Positive</u>: Sensitivity. Kindness. Intuition. Friendship. Romanticism. Patience. Calm. The desire to help others.
<u>Negative</u>: Nervous weakness. The betrayal of a friend. Naivety.

QUEEN OF PENTACLES

<u>Positive</u>: A woman who loves money and who has financial means. Materialism. A generous person with friends or loved ones. Search for profitability. You keep your feet on the ground.
<u>Negative</u>: Fear of failure. Calculating and scheming attitude. Bad financial investments.

QUEEN OF SWORDS
<u>Positive</u>: Authority. A very direct speech. Independence. Prudence. Acumen. Determination.
<u>Negative</u>: Widowhood or divorce. Conflicts. Emotional dryness. Wickedness. Financial difficulties. Stubbornness.

QUEEN OF WANDS
<u>Positive</u>: Great self-confidence. Lucidity (especially in the financial and professional fields). Success. Well-lived sexuality.
<u>Negative</u>: Jealousy. Authoritarianism. Pride.

THE KINGS
Authority. Hierarchy. The leader. Competence. Loyalty. Power. Stability.
The querent, the husband, the partner.

of Cups	of Pentacles	of Swords	of Wands

KING OF CUPS
<u>Positive</u>: Creativity. Constancy. Generosity. Trust. The control over emotions. Spirituality.
<u>Negative</u>: Cunning. Bad financial surprises. Emotional blackmail.

KING OF PENTACLES
<u>Positive</u>: Stable and meticulous. A material and financial base. The responsibilities. The habits and the routine.
<u>Negative</u>: Too strong a taste for money. Excessive spending. Too sure of one's rights.

KING OF SWORDS
<u>Positive</u>: Intelligence. Analytical mind. Authority. Accuracy of judgement. High level of demand.
<u>Negative</u>: Tyranny. Cruelty. Revenge. Narrow-mindedness.

KING OF WANDS
<u>Positive</u>: Power. Vitality. Enthusiasm. Professional and social success. Soul of a leader.
<u>Negative</u>: Selfishness. Overambitious, intriguing. Incapable of emotion, coldness. Intolerance.

3 - THE GENERIC CARDS AND THEIR CARDS OF SUBSTITUTION (OR REPLACEMENT)

To use the Tarot correctly, it is essential to learn the meaning of the 22 major arcanas. Remembering two or three words for each of the cards is a good way to start. The more you practice, the more your vocabulary will naturally grow. It is also important to know the cards that represent the major areas of a human being's life.

A generic card is one that primarily represents an area of life. For example, The Chariot is the generic (therefore priority) arcana of work.
Other cards, called substitution or replacement, may replace The Chariot in the context of a work issue, if it is not present in the draw.
It is necessary to remember that generic arcanas are always stronger than their replacements.

WORK
Generic card: The Chariot(VII)
<u>Substitute card</u>: The Emperor (IIII), for its capacity for structure and Hermit (VIIII) for perseverance and meticuloussness. Death (XIII) which represents labor, hard work.

FINANCES
Generic card: The Devil (XV)
<u>Substitute card:</u> The Emperor (IIII) also for the material, The Tower (XVI) for the capacity for material surprises, or The Wheel of Fortune (X), for the possibility of finances to come. These two last cards are not very powerful financially, we must carefully study the whole draw.

EMOTION
Generic card: The Lovers (VI)
<u>Substitute card</u>: The Sun (XVIIII) which represents, amongst other things, the couple, The Hierophant (V) whose concerns are unions, or The Hanged Man (XII) who can speak of emotional bonds.

HEALTH
Generic card: The Hanged Man (XII)
<u>Substitute card</u>: The Star (XVII), which is closely connected with all bodily questions, The Fool (XXII), which represents the human being in its bodily and psychological entirety, and Death (XIII), which symbolizes sudden physical problems and bodily mutations too.

These generic arcanas and their replacements are to be learned perfectly, as they enable you to act faster and with more certainty on your projections.

MAKING THE CARDS SPEAK: PHRASING

After years of teaching, I have noticed that the greatest difficulty encountered by the apprentice is to succeed in "making the Tarot speak" simply and effectively. How to tell the story proposed by a draw? How to choose the words according to the cards in action? How do you express your feelings or ideas?

Just like an alphabet, the Tarot takes on its full dimension when the different arcanas meet. It then becomes possible to read the associations to deliver the right message.

Example for a professional question: a man asks if he will find work soon.

- the first card drawn is The Magician (1): Something new seems to happen but it is not enough to affirm anything.
- the second card drawn is The Chariot (7): This is a very good sign since it is the generic arcana for work.
- the third card drawn is The Devil (15): It is the generic arcana of money but it also represents power. The association of these three cards could be read as: «*Your draw is positive, you will find a new (1) job (7) that is lucrative (15)*». *It is also possible to read the cards out of order: "You will earn money (15) thanks to a new (1) job (7)".*

To familiarize yourself with the phrasing, it is advisable to start slowly, with two cards. As your understanding progresses, you can add several cards to make increasingly detailed and precise phrasings.

Examples of phrasing with two cards:

9 / 7: an old (9) car (7)
1 / 18: a new (1) house (18)
14 / 19: vacation (14) in summer (19)
14 / 18: vacation (14) in winter (18)
7 / 22: a foreign (22) car (7). This configuration can also mean a job (7) abroad (22).

Examples of phrasing with three cards:

1 / 19 / 2: a child (1) brilliant (19) in studies (2)
14 / 6 / 1: the return (14) of a love (6) of youth (1)
3 / 6 / 4: a woman (3) in love (6) with a man (4)
18 / 16 / 19: a move (18 / 16) to the south (19).

Examples of phrasings with four cards:

1 / 6 / 21 / 7: a new (1) love encounter (6) in the professional (7) world (21)
4 / 3 / 18 / 20: a man (4) meets a woman (3) in a disco (18/20: a house 18 of music 20)
21/22/19/17: a trip abroad (21/22) next (17) summer (19).

When you think you understand how to phrase a reading, you can practice draws for you or your loved ones.

4 - READINGS

THE RULES FOR PRACTICING THE TAROT WELL

When working with the Tarot, the attitude to adopt as well as the "rules" to follow are always the same:
- find inner calm, as much as possible.
- choose a time of day when you will not be disturbed.
- during a draw, ask a very specific question, which will naturally give a specific answer. It is not advisable to ask, for example: «*Will I be rich one day?*» but rather to formulate: « *How will my financial situation evolve in the near future?* ».
- carry out a single draw for a question.
Even if you don't like the result, there's no need to start over right away. Keep the answer in mind for the weeks to come.
- agree to be wrong.
If you have made an error in analysis and interpretation, look again at the draw and you will realize that the Tarot indicated precisely what happened. Personal questioning is essential, especially at the start of learning! You will always learn more from failure than from victory.
-be careful if you make a draw for someone, everyone receives words with a different sensitivity.

The Tarot should not be a tool that causes stress or presents a bad omen, but a tool of help.
- you can practice the Tarot any day and at any time, as long as you do it seriously and as a way to provide help to others.

THE CUT READING

This is the most accessible draw, it answers specific questions perfectly. In its one-level formula (the one we are going to study), its space-time does not exceed three months.

To practice the cut, you must first quietly shuffle the Universal Grand Tarot upright, breathe in deeply, while concentrating on your question. When you are ready, lay out your deck in front of you, facing down. Choose two cards while still thinking about your question.

Turn over the first selected card and place it on the left. It represents the positive part of your question, your assets, your strengths or your abilities to face the subject concerned; we call it the **"for"** (A).

Then turn over the second card you have chosen and place it on the right. It represents the negative part of your question, your weaknesses, what you are lacking or your problems; we call it the **"against"** (B).

The way to interpret this is very easy:
If the generic card of the studied area appears in «for», the answer to the question you are asking is positive. If the generic card of the studied area appears in «against», the answer is negative.

When no generic card appears in your draw, it is necessary to calculate the occult arcana (we will talk about this later).

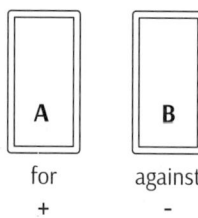

for   against
+   -

1 - THE SIMPLE CUT

Example : « *Am I going to find work ?* »
The cut: (7 / 1 - The Chariot and The Magician)

+   -

The generic card is in «for», the answer is therefore favorable. Here is the interpretation:
"you will find work very quickly (7, in favor) in the next three to four weeks. Don't be afraid to go for it (1, against)!"

2 - THE ONE LEVEL CUT

To get more details and go further in time, just practice the cut at one level. This makes it possible to explore the coming three months and better understand the mechanisms of success or blockages in the draw, thanks to the calculations of the occult arcanas.

An occult arcana is the result of the addition of two cards, without needing to draw other cards.

The Tarot cards are numbered from 1 (The Magician) to 22 (The Fool). When two cards are added, the sum obtained must not exceed 22.

<u>Demonstration</u>: by adding the Hierophant (5) and The Sun (19), we obtain 24: 2 + 4 make 6. The occult arcana obtained is The Lovers (6).
On the other hand, if we add The Moon (18) and The Emperor (4), we get 22, which is The Fool.

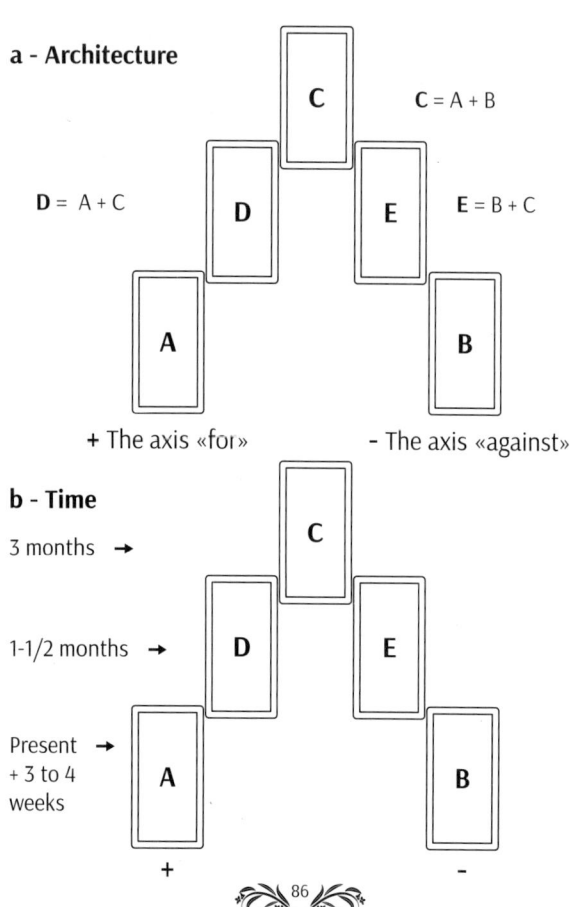

Let's go back to our example: *"Will I find a job?"*. <u>The cut</u>: 7 / 1. The one-level cut will allow us to further develop our answer by placing the different information in time.

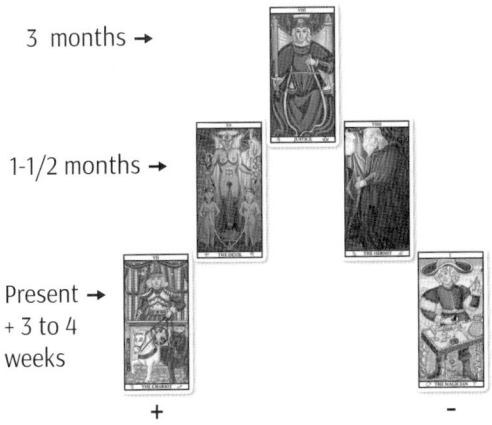

3 months →

1-1/2 months →

Present →
+ 3 to 4
weeks

+   -

Here is the interpretation: *"You will very quickly find work (7, The Chariot in favor) within 3 to 4 weeks to come. Do not be afraid to start (1, The Magician in "against"). This work will be lucrative (15, The Devil) and you will also obtain, in 3 months, a stable contract (8, Justice)"*. It is also possible to say: *"You will obtain (8) a professional contract (7) that is lucrative (15)"*. Thanks to the occult arcanas, we know that this person will earn his living properly in 1-1/2 months because The Devil, the generic card of finances, intervenes in this time period.

This draw is reassuring because it shows a natural progression of a person finding work, earning a living and confirming their position.

In the case of a positive response like here, it is necessary to minimize the message of the against' axis (1 - 9 - 8); The Magician indicates that one should not be afraid to start or make a mistake and The Hermit advises against excessive shyness.

2nd Example: *"Am I going to move?"* A man asks the question. The cut: (13- 5: Death - The Hierophant). The occult arcanas give this :

+   -

<u>What the visual of the cards evokes</u>: this cut inspires work, will and speed. The presence of The Emperor on the positive axis is an excellent sign, it indicates an active man, willing and wishing to act and bring his project to life. Death (13), also in this same time period, immediately shows a change of importance and a quick action. Finally, The Moon (18), the generic card of dwelling (of the question) is present: the move (13/18) will take place quickly (13) thanks to his will (4). On the positive axis, the association of Death and The Emperor literally indicates: "a favorable change (13) for a man (4), concerning a dwelling (18, The Moon). The answer to this question is positive: this man will find a new home in about three months, as indicated by the positioning of The Moon in the draw.

*Note: *it is important to minimize the "against" as well as the negative axis, when the answer to the question is clearly indicated on the positive axis.* **The cut draw answers a specific question but it is also an overall instantaneous "photograph" of the querent's life.** *The negative axis can then evoke other areas of his life.*

For example, we know that this man will not need the help of a real estate agent because the typical configuration for this profession (5/18: a real estate specialist) appears on the negative axis of the draw.

THE CROSS READING

The cross reading (also called the draw in five) is the most used Tarologist's technique. Its structured architecture and its precise temporal space make it an easy draw, while being visually pleasing.

With study and practice, you can achieve excellent results.

This draw allows a projection over approximately 8 to 10 months. To practice, simply lay out the Tarot, face down, then select 5 cards by asking your question. As with the cut draw, some meanings have to be memorized:

- Look to see if the consultant (4, The Emperor or 3, The Empress) appears in the draw. Their presence indicates action, willpower and often success.

- See if a card pertaining to the question asked is present, for example The Chariot (7) for work, The Lovers (6) for love, The Devil (15) for money... A generic card in a favorable position is always a good sign.

- Check that the present time truly corresponds to the current situation of the querent or that the cards drawn are related to the question asked.

a) - Architecture and time of the cross draw

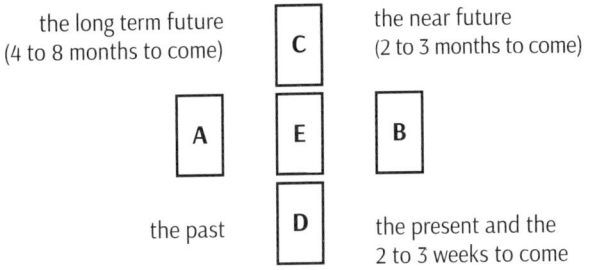

It is then enough to set up the calculations in order to obtain a maximum of information.

A = first card drawn; B = second card drawn; C = third card drawn; D = fourth card drawn; E = fifth card drawn.
F = Axis of the past (A + D) ; G = Axis of the present (D + B); H = Axis of the near future (B + C); I = Axis of the long term future(C+A).
J = Diagonal axis of the past (F+E); K = Diagonal axis of the present (G+E); L = Diagonal axis of the near future (H+E); M = Diagonal axis of the long term future (I+E)

Example: *"I want to study so I can work in the fashion industry (clothing, haute couture). Will I get a place in the school of my choice?* – A woman asks the question.

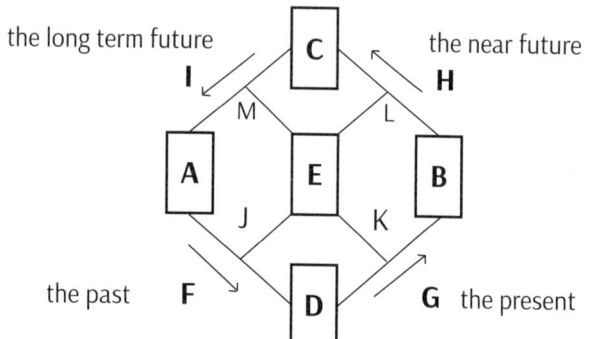

The first sensation: The generic card of studies (2: The High Priestess) is at the center of the draw. This is all the more encouraging as many positive cards strengthen and harmonize the whole (4/15/11/10/8/7/13). In these excellent conditions, the absence of The Empress, 3 (who represents the querent) is not a worry.

The visual of the cards and the technical particularities of the draw: The draw is both dynamic and voluntary (4 / 7 / 11). The High Priestess evokes seriousness and reflection; The Star (17), the card that represents the arts in general, brings a lot of hope.

Study of the past sector: The studies (2) have been followed, so far, seriously (4) and with mastery and self-confidence (11). They have been a crowning success (7). This woman has sometimes experienced difficult periods in her studies (13/2) but she has managed to structure herself correctly (4/11). Her desire to do specialized (2) work (7) of a manual nature (13) is not recent. She has had a real desire for professional (7) mastery (11) for some time.

Study of the present sector: The querent is strong-willed (11/4), she knows what she wants (4) and she gives herself the means (11). Her sense of aesthetics (17) and her passion (15) for the fashion profession ensure her a place in this school (2).

Study of the near future: Studies (2) for a job related to beauty (17).The querent will give herself the means (11) to evolve (10), even if it will require some sacrifices (12). It's a bit like going into religion (2/12).

Study of the long term future: Studies (2) balancing (8) and pleasant (6). Studies (2) which will bring in the future (17) a job (7). **How to phrase the reading:**

"You wanted to do these studies for a long time (2). You gave yourself all the means (4/11) and even if you have sometimes experienced moments of depression (13) in your school path (2), you never gave up (11/4) and you never stopped moving forward with determination (7/4).
Your desire to do a highly skilled job (7/13/2: manual work requiring great knowledge) is strong (11).
You are completely right to believe in it and to hope (17), your passion (15) for the world of fashion, your will and your courage (4/11) will allow you to obtain a place (4) in this school (2). Your studies will start well (2/10), your self-confidence will make you move forward (11/10) toward your vocation (12) for an artistic profession (17), even if you have to make some sacrifices (12/17). This school path will bring you great satisfaction (6), you will find your balance (8) and your professional fulfillment in this work (17/7/2)".

Go beyond the question asked: reassign a draw

Knowing how to reassign a draw means allowing yourself to feel and express something else than the question asked. It means "navigating" with all cards in action to talk about another area or another person. Always showing great understanding and care.

Please note that not all draws can be reassigned. Follow your instincts and keep it simple; especially when you have already obtained clear answers to the question asked or the area studied.

In the case of an sensitive analysis for this women, you will notice, in the present sector: 4 / 15 / 17 / 11: very physical cards that indicate a great sexual passion (15/11) and physical (17) with a man (4) she meets secretly (2). While continuing this sensitive analysis, you will notice that The Lovers (generic card for love) is present in this draw, surrounded by 17/6/7/8/2.

<u>The analysis can be done as follows:</u>
"Within 8 to 10 months (the future, 17 is placed on the sector of the far future), you will make a romantic encounter (6) of high quality (6/7/17). This story will be balanced (8) and emotionally harmonious (6/17)".

ABOUT THE AUTHOR

Dear Reader,

Here we have arrived at the end of this book. I hope it will have allowed you to discover the Tarot in another way and to enrich your knowledge and skills.
With practice, you can experiment with the Grand Universal Tarot and find your own way of working with it.
I wish for you, evolution in love, light and brotherhood.

— Bruno de Nys

Scan the QR code below to visit the author's YouTube channel to learn more.